Library of Congress Cataloging-in-Publication Data

Powell, Richard, (date)
    Babies / words by Richard Powell; pictures by Alan Snow.
       p.   cm.—(A Child's practical guide)
    Cover title: How to deal with babies.
    Summary: A boy describes his adjustment to the arrival of his baby sister and how he learned to get along with her and enjoy her company.
    ISBN 0-8167-2420-2 (lib. bdg.)   ISBN 0-8167-2421-0 (pbk.)
    1. Infants—Juvenile literature. 2. Infants—Development—Juvenile literature. [1. Babies. 2. Brothers and sisters.]
I. Snow, Alan, ill. II. Title. III. Title: How to deal with babies. IV. Series: Powell, Richard, 1957-   Child's practical guide.
HQ774.P68 1992
305.23 '2—dc20   91-3461

Published by Watermill Press.
Produced for Watermill Press by Joshua Morris Publishing, Inc.
in association with Treehouse Children's Books Ltd.
Illustrations copyright © 1990 Alan Snow.
Text copyright © 1990 Treehouse Children's Books Ltd.
All rights reserved.
Text printed in Singapore. Cover printed in U.S.A.
Bound in U.S.A.
10 9 8 7 6 5 4 3 2 1

How to Deal with BABIES

Words by Richard Powell
Pictures by Alan Snow

WATERMILL PRESS

One day my mom told me I was going to have a baby brother . . . or sister. "Where does it come from?" I asked. "It's growing inside of me," she said. That made me laugh.

But she did get very big.   She went to the hospital . . .

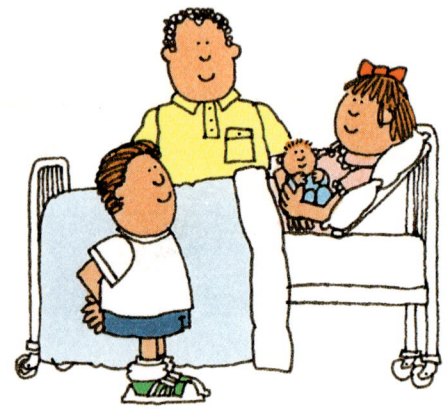

and there was a baby!   It was very noisy . . .

and naughty!

Mom loved it.

Now my sister Beth is my best friend. She's bigger now, and she plays with me. We get along fine . . . most of the time. If you have a baby in your house, here's how to make friends . . .

"Can't we call it Batman?"

When Dad and I went to see Mom in the hospital, she was glad to see us. I had missed her. She showed me my new baby sister. I said she was pretty, because everybody else did. Mom said the baby's name was Beth.

"5...4...3...2...1..."

The hospital was a bit scary and very big. I took some toys along, but I'm not sure it was a good idea. Mom said perhaps I should be quieter, and play when I got home.

"This is Eddie. He's yours."

It was a great day when Mom brought Beth home.
Everybody wanted to see her. I was glad
Mom was home. I gave my best teddy bear to Beth.
Mom was pleased. *Everybody* said how good I was.

"Waaaaaaagh!"

When baby Beth cried, everybody fussed over her!
Mom said Beth was too little to talk.
"She cries to tell us something is wrong," Mom said.
Poor Beth! It must be horrible not to be able to talk.

"Here are some more diapers, Mom."

I watched Mom change baby Beth. She was so tiny. "She needs looking after," said Mom. I helped get the diapers ready. I like helping to look after her, because *I'm* big, and *she's* so small.

"Isn't she strong, Mom?"

I put my finger in baby Beth's hand, and she held it. It felt funny, but nice. Her fingers were small, but very strong. I was glad to have a sister who was so strong.

I like noise. But baby Beth needed to sleep a lot, so she could grow big enough to play with me. That's what my mom says. I tried not to wake her, but sometimes I forgot . . .

"Ouch! Ouch! Ouch!"

Baby Beth did grow strong enough to play with me. She grew bigger, and she grew teeth. Watch out when babies grow teeth . . . they bite.

I used to get mad at Beth, because she started to help herself . . . to *my* toys.

She soon learned to crawl . . . and help herself.

She soon learned to stand . . . and help herself.

She soon learned to walk . . . and help herself.

So I learned to share, and now we get along . . .

"YEEOW!"

. . . except when she won't let go!
Mom says I shouldn't get mad, and that Beth is too small to understand.
I'm not so sure.

"More, more, more, more, MORE!"

Because she's so small, Beth can't feed herself.
I help.
Beth loves it when I help.

"Mom, can Beth eat creepy crawlies?"

Mom says that because Beth is my little sister, I should look after her. I often get Beth into trouble, like when she puts little things in her mouth. Mom says they could choke her.

Beth and I love to play . . .

hide-and-seek . . .

house . . .

doctor . . .

anything!

I love my sister Beth.